JOSTLING WITH
THE PEARS

by

SANDRA SAER

illustrated in colour,
and with two original drawings
by EUAN DUNN

To all I love –

My family,
especially Nathaniel Henry Saer,
wondrously born one St Valentine's Day;

My friends,
especially Patrick Moore and Janet Carter,
and friends around no longer;

and

For all those things that have been
my inspiration to write, throughout my life,

- I give my thanks.

Contents

Preface

1. MOON; LORD 1

2. HELPING EACH OTHER OUT 2

3. THE FALLOWING 4

4. ANOTHER TIME, ANOTHER PLACE 7

5. TALKING TO GROWING THINGS.......................... 9

6. A PRIMROSE-COVERED STEP............................ 12

7. IT'S NEVER TOO LATE 13

8. FOR JULIA 15

9. FRIENDS AND RELATIONS 17

10. ON A LOVELY SUMMER EVENING...................... 19

11. JOSTLING WITH THE PEARS............................. 21

12. PRESENTS 23

13. *REAL* TRUE GRIT 24

14. ENCOUNTER WITH AN OLD ROBIN 26

15. ONCE UPON A TIME 28

16. YOU'RE A STAR 33

17. WINTER COMES.. 35

PREFACE

Why Jostling? you may wonder.

In his *GNOMIC VERSES*, William Blake wrote:

> *Great things are done when men and mountains meet;*
> *this is not done by jostling in the street.*

That may be important to some, and acceptable to others,
but it is not how I think about jostling.

The word engages me with people, friendship; love; in the possibility of
being helpful to someone – in the street, or wherever it may be.

In other words, my jostling involves me with communication.

In the third, and final therefore, part of my Pear Tree Cottage anthology,
I acknowledge my huge debt to living there, sharing life with my children
growing up and our animals, good neighbours and, of course, with my
former, unforgettable, church community in Coldwaltham.

So this is a kind of cathartic 'goodbye to all that', which is very difficult
to make. It was been a wonderful, exciting, at times worrying but
ultimately, rewarding period in my life. Time now to move on.

I hope you may find pleasure, and pause for personal reflection in these
writings.

Sandra Saer
Arundel
2012

1

Moon; Lord

What is this moon,
mingling through darkness
to light,

cruising through clouds
to shine?
hope in the night?

Hope, bringing grace
in a worrying world,
facing the plight of wars
we never imagined would happen;
would never be involved in.

And so, Moon, Lord,
we look up and see You,
cruising through clouds,
to shine, and give us all
Hope in the Night.

This poem was written a few days after the '9/11' tragedy (11 September, 2001), but it would seem to be relevant to all the continuing wars and battles for power since then. I had been looking up at the sky above the cottage, after watering my garden in the moonlight.

2

Helping each other out

Watching an excellent Channel 4 television programme a long time ago, about the 1987 hurricane and the City market crash in London, reminded me of that and other times when we have had to face the need – the compulsion, to help each other out.

When that more or less unexpected hurricane smashed in on us, there were instantly people in our community, as in many others, trying to help as best we could. No power, so those of us with solid-fuel Rayburn stoves set up soup kitchens. Getting independent old people to accept what some considered as 'charity' was difficult. Coaxing them to contact us was even more difficult! In the end, however, we did help many people, and they were grateful. That gratitude was reward enough. One of our few failures was with an elderly parishioner who, when I went to see her, said I needn't have bothered – she had a camp stove fixed up in her garage!

During and just after World War 2, helping one another was something all those families round me – then a small child in rural North Wales – did, and did without question. If we had bread and the Hayes family next door didn't, and asked my mother for some, she would give it to them, without hesitation. At the time, she received coupons worth one and a quarter loaves a day – for a family of five. I never heard her complain.

At the age of ten, I remember biking a mile, at seven in the morning, up to a market garden, where I queued, in the hope of buying a pound of tomatoes to have on toast for breakfast. I did this many times, without a fuss. When I was unlucky because the tomatoes had run out, I biked back, dejected.

"Never mind, darling," was all Mummy would say, "We'll have marmite on toast instead."

Then came the Tsunami. In a splendid, re-scheduled 'Songs of Praise' on BBC 1 that January, we learnt how those who had survived the disaster just got on with helping each other. No hysteria. No whingeing. Just the need to keep things as near to normal as possible. And those who went out from other countries to help, behaved likewise.

This need for mutual care should be – no, is – a timeless one. Organisations like Christian Aid and Make Poverty History REMIND us of this need.

3

The Fallowing

Allotment holders, with a limited amount of space, tend to plant and seed it with the produce they wish to grow and harvest. That said, the savvy ones often choose to leave a small patch bare, and use it again the next year, or the year after.

With one-third of an acre of garden at Pear Tree Cottage, it was something of a relief to leave a *big* patch bare. I usually did this, for most of my 27 years stewarding the space, growing crops in the rest of the un-grassed areas in a three-year rotation.

That all sounds clever and organised, but staring down at a piece of ground only slightly sprinkled with weeds, I was often tempted to throw something in there.

Many years ago, the old shoe repairer in Arundel suggested just using a bit of the fallow land.

"Just dig a big hole, and chuck in some potatoes. Cut 'em in half if you're short – and cover 'em up well. You'll get a fine crop."

The horticultural purists might not approve of this, but it works! And by the time you've washed, and boiled, roasted or fried the potatoes, what 'nasties' could there be in them?

In general, though, leaving land fallow is a good notion. Richness in the earth has a chance to re-assert itself; useful worms delve, undisturbed. If nettle beds are left untouched, the bees and

---

butterflies will be delighted. (And soup made with young nettles is delicious, as one of my neighbours taught me.)

Nevertheless, the three-year rotation of crops requires not only a good memory (do we all write down what we grew in different plots in the previous year?), but annual pre-organisation.

Some of the vegetables we grow don't appear to be in the groups they're supposed to be in. We err sometimes. (Where did those parsnips come from? I don't remember planting them *there*. And these spring onions have appeared in quite the wrong place, too…)

In much the same way, it is a good idea to let our minds lie fallow from time to time. Certainly, in my case, it works. I suddenly realise I've run out of thoughts, ideas. It could be alarming to one (not just me) whose mind races along at a vast rate of knots. But it is essential, however difficult it may prove to be.

*****

This was written as I sat at the open window of my log-cabin suite at a hotel high up in the Madeira mountains. I grew so relaxed, I could have lain down and slept, or just rested, on and on.

It had taken me two days, though, to get to a blissful, blank-minded, slow-moving state, having completed a difficult twelve-hour journey from home to reach this magnificent mountainous place, with huge peaks rising up dramatically before me, and terraced gardens full of brilliant flowers below. (How they manage to reach the slopes around to sow and reap, I have no idea, but good crops were growing there.)

A further two days were needed before I could cease wondering WHAT I SHOULD BE DOING? hour by hour. On the fourth day, I finally stopped worrying about anything – except if there'd still be left the thick, creamy, hotel-made yoghourt, with which to begin each gargantuan breakfast!

Warm sunshine, the gush of rock springs, a cock who crowed incessantly (he's not unique: I had one just like that, next to the cottage). No need to do anything; go anywhere.

Mmmmmm. Think I'll just have a snooze...

4

Another Time, another Place

During my lovely Madeira trip (see Chapter 3), I left my log-cabin suite high-up in the mountains and descended to Funchal, the capital, for two days. One reason was that I wanted to find Holy Trinity, the Anglican Church, and attend its mid-morning Sunday Service, on my last day.

With difficulty I found the church, tucked away in a maze of side streets. But it was worth the perseverance. The joyful Service, in a large church (packed mainly with English visitors) started with an absorbing excerpt from a diary* written by an English lady, Isabella Hurst. At 57, she married a 50-year-old Madeiran landowner, Henriques de Franca. They had their honeymoon in Funchal, arriving on 15 August, 1853, and spent almost a year there, before returning to England.

The diary entry, read with gusto by Tony Hughes-Lewis, one of the churchwardens, was as follows (the capitals and semi-colons are all Isabella's!):

'On the 21st August, I went to (the Anglican) Church for the first time in Madeira, my Husband taking me to the door, and meeting me again when I came out; but my surprise at the assembling of the congregation was extreme. As there are many streets in Funchal which deserve the name of Break-back Street, besides that in which the Church stands; and as the City is very large, and people of course live in every part of it; and as there were no wheel carriages; the ladies go to the Church, some in Cars drawn by oxen, some in Palanquins (palanquin: a covered litter for one, usually carried by four or six men!!) or Hammocks, and some on horseback; many of the latter in white veils, silk mantillas or lace cloaks, and white or coloured muslin dresses, flounced above the knees; the flounces flying out from the saddle in the most ludicrous manner, for they do not trouble themselves to wear habits unless they intend to ride some distance. Some of the ladies had a large linen petticoat, which was put on like an apron hind part before, to preserve their dresses, which was slipped off at the Church door, and given in charge to the man who runs beside the horses, in his white trousers, blue jacket, and pointed cap, stuck on the top of his head, with its long tail standing upright. Altogether the scene was so truly ludicrous, and the trampling of the horses, the noise of the ox cars, the ringing or rather jingling of the bells around the necks of the oxen, the only bells we have, for we must not have Church bells, and the mingled cries of the drivers, the half English, half Portuguese phrases on all sides, made such a babel of noises that it was certainly the most un-Churchlike scene I have ever witnessed, and it took several Sundays before I could believe that I was not going to a Fair.'

*****

One can well imagine that!! Fortunately, on the day of the Service I went to, most of us arrived quietly, by car or on foot…S.S.

*A Journal of a Visit to Madeira 1853-1854 (Junta Geral de Distrito Autonomo do Funchal. 1969 (now, sadly, out of print)

5

Talking to Growing Things

M y neighbours were used to me wandering round the garden, dead-heading, and snapping off odd twigs as I went; talking out loud.

– There she goes again! Must be a good bit of dialogue, that, she's been at it for half an hour!

They thought I was working out parts for a play – seeing how one would speak to another, in a given situation. Often, they were right.

But sometimes I was just talking to trees and plants. A runner bean stem looking sickly, for example, while the rest growing round the wigwam were forging ahead.

"Come on," I'd say, encouragingly, "buck up!" Sometimes I even got cross ...

One companion on my garden tours was a pheasant. He had arrived, without ceremony, one day - and stayed. I called him Ian, after a late, dear friend.

Ian's favourite place was on the patio, a rudimentary but adequate construction of cement paving slabs, installed by Fred, for Gordon Turrell, a River Lane neighbour. It took me a long time to understand why he preferred the patio. One day I found him staring into what I first thought was the cottage back wall, then realised there was a mirror against the wall (goodness knows how it got there). Ian often stood before the mirror. Eventually I realised he saw in the reflection another pheasant.

– What a fine fellow! he probably thought …

Anyway, I liked his company, and we grew attached, possibly because I put good grain out for him to eat each day, while I was having my breakfast inside, and quietly chatted to him on our walkabouts.

There was a family pear tree that didn't seem to want to bring forth fruit, except for the odd, full-bodied Comice. It was planted alongside my Conference pear tree (the one that inspired this book). Unlike its neighbour, which refused to stop growing, even after being pruned virtually to the ground, the family pear tree drooped sadly, blossomed badly, and this went on for three years.

One day, in Spring, I stood before the tree and gave it a good talking-to.

"Now look here," I said – out loud.

"How's the play going, Sandra?" enquired a neighbour from the lane, walking her dog.

"Fine," I replied briefly, turning back to the tree. I let the neighbour disappear out of sight. Then

"Now look here!" I repeated, sternly, "it's time you started giving me some nice pears – this summer, if you don't mind. One Comice, one Conference (bigger and better than your neighbouring tree) and one William … Big, juicy fruit. What do you say?"

Somewhat worried that I had been too harsh, I stroked the tree gently (non one was looking, but what if they were!). I caressed the trunk, the branches, the knobbly little twigs, and said quietly that I would look forward to the blossom forming.

Rather like the sleeping princess in 'Snow White and the Seven Dwarfs', perhaps the tree took this in. I couldn't be sure. No blossom appeared.

But next Spring, about to start remonstrating again, I observed tiny pin pricks of blossom emerging from obliging twigs. The blossom turned pale pink … The pears formed. That late summer, my sleeping tree, awakened by Nature's Prince, produced a lovely Comice pear and a pretty good Conference one.

I expect I'll get more fruit next year. Even a William, maybe.

6

A Primrose-covered Step

Your poem is of a special day,
long years ago,
but clear as yesterday
in your young mind:
Grandad Pete; a go-cart;
his 'warm belly, warm breath';
a shared, loving nearness.

You say the memory is too late.
'It's over now.'
No. Wait!
Such moments help to form
the firm fabric of our lives.

A good memory is like
a fragrant, primrose-covered step
up from the past,
into the present.

Such God-grace lift-ups
also lead us
into love-filled futures.
There, Lily,
I hope that you will be.

** *written in January 2007 for Lily Dunsford, when aged 11*

7

It's never too late ...

We gardeners*, who mop our brows in an early-summer heatwave, having watched our plants and seedlings wilt – in some cases wither – in an abnormally cold spring, can now be glad we were late with our plantings. And then – the blessed rain ...

The Gardening Section of Saturday's DAILY TELEGRAPH is full of good advice. Occasionally, the Gardening Gurus don't necessarily get it right. I remember one of my neighbours once remarking scornfully that much of the GG's advice is no news to us. Country mores and experienced husbandry helped us along.

In mid-June, we were told that it was much too late to plant pepper seeds. Nonsense! I said out loud, at the kitchen table. I had put mine in a week before and already small green heads of shoots were poking out of the compost. Three days later, the shoots were small plants, preening themselves as they grew strongly on, in back-porch heat.

Many years ago, Orlando, my youngest son, was involved in a production at his school, Bradfield College, of *The Boyfriend*, Sandy Wilson's jolly frolic of a musical. One of the songs was sung by a fifteen-year-old, dressed up to appear sixty-ish, with hair powdered white! In a clear young voice, he sang 'It's never too late to fall in love'. (Some of us hope it isn't!)

One thing is certain. It's never too late to try to love people, even if they appear to be unlovable or unapproachable. Somewhere, if we accept the challenge to look, there is a chink in the emotional armour of many we find it difficult to even *like*.

At a past bookselling event, one of my customers fell, for a long time, into the that category. No smile, a terse request for a book he held out, the money for it thrown down on the table. I got fed up with it! On one occasion, he wanted a book of poetry. He held it out to me, gaze averted.

I cleared my throat. "You would like to buy this book?"

"Yes," he said, gruffly.

"Thank you," I said with a sweet smile. "I'll put it in a bag for you. Here you are."

He had to say "thank you" back, didn't he? *Communication had begun!*

"Do you like poetry?" I asked.

"Yes," he replied, shyly. "And – (getting enthused) and I write it."

"That's wonderful. I write poetry, too. That's my book!"

This produced the response I was angling for. And his smile was the start of a warm friendship.

* *sadly, I have no garden now, in Arundel. But some memories don't fade.*

For Julia

In a cool wind,
the roses
have strewn their petals down
for you
in pale pink, fragrant drops of tears
to join my own;
mine drop with the rain
that smears
everything in this garden
you have known.

Friendship is strange sometimes,
begotten among strangers
not seeking it.
We – you and Colin and I –
were friends from the beginning;
with lives that seemed to fit
one with the others.

You now live
where others might
their eye teeth give
for just one more
sweet glimpse of you.

But there you are,
and we are here,
smiling at your memory,
with many a pale pink, petal tear.

9 July 2008

Children camping at Lodge Hill Centre (just up the road), drawing the Cottage façade, before orange squash and biscuits from the kitchen

The path into the Cottage garden

A view of my productive garden

Another garden view, of 'O' for Orlando, planted in lettuce round some self-seeded Golden Rod!

Sandra and Fred, with Tan-Tan, Fred's lookalike, and master

Fred sailing joyfully over the back gate, to greet children just home from school

Sandra with Fruitie, our West County cat, and Fred — on guard!

*Libby with Charis
and baby Barnaby*

Bella with Greenie, her favourite cat, 1st prize winner at Coldwaltham Village Fete

Barbecue days: Orlando and Charis at PTC's annual celebration

Friends reunited at the Pear Tree Cottage barbecue

The Cottage sitting room, with Grandfather MH's clock in central position, and Mother's Day flowers in the Sussex stone fireplace

Small Amelia and Thomas Saer, relaxing in the sitting room

The kitchen dresser, decked for Christmas around Uncle Michael's gift of a magnificent blue and gold crib from Venezuela

Later: The Anguses: Angus with Thomas, Tor with Isabel, Amelia and Bella, in a hug

An arch of Morning Glory, strung between two wigwams of beans, with Besleys Farm in the background

My great friend, Stan Ruff, with his long-time friend, Jim Secomb

9

... Friends and Relations

Recently, I received an email from Facebook, informing me that Alasdhair, my Godson and nephew, wished to add me to his profile – as a friend.

I was especially moved, since he and I had been trying to make up for lost years of not knowing each other. So it was encouraging to know Alasdhair considered me as a friend, as well as a relation.

What a train of thought *that* set off!

Many years ago, Orlando, when very young indeed, gave me a present wrapped in coloured paper featuring old samplers. The text carefully and purposely centred on the front of the parcel read:

> *Tell me, ye knowing and discerning few*
> *Where I may find a friend both firm and true*
> *Who dares stand by me when in deep distress*
> *And then his love and friendship most express.*

It was this same son who told me of a recent family death, his filial comfort and hug laced with exactly the kind of friendship described on the wrapping paper.

Friends. Do we value them sufficiently? I'm sure many of us do, without thinking about it. But we *need* to think about it, because of their intrinsic value in our lives. In our community, as in many others, there is a special concentration of warm friendship. How lucky we are to have it!

Sometimes, friends mean more to us than relatives. It has been said many times that we choose our friends, but not our relatives.

When my beloved dog, Fred, died of a heart attack, while out on his evening stroll up the hill from River Lane, I was bereft. With the children gone, he was such a wonderful companion. If I was sad, he knew, and would rest his head on my knee, looking soulfully up at me. When I was happy, we would go out into the garden and he would race round and round and round it, to celebrate my mood.

Before that, he had been our *family* friend, and I have a precious photograph of him leaping, joyfully, clean over the back garden gate, each time the children came back for the school holidays.

When he died, I wrapped Fred in the duvet my neighbour had provided as a shroud. Barley's David buried him in the garden, in the shelter of the honeysuckle hedge. As I looked on, I remember thinking darkly how much more I had loved him than certain other members of my family. Quite wrong, I'm sure, but I *did* think it.

The thing about friendship is that it is an unconditional expression of affection and encouragement – and isn't encouragement one of the finest forms of love?

10

On a Lovely Summer Evening

On a lovely summer evening
we were there to have a meeting
in my Pear Tree Cottage kitchen.
All looked down upon the table
where our parish map lay, finished,
celebrating the Millennium.
Suddenly we all heard voices;
shouting, laughing, high-pitched-voices.
Round the door peeped Annie Nelson
and her children, Rhys and Phoebe.

Consternation from the others
hoping for a quiet discussion.
Quick now! What was I to do?

"Rhys and Phoebe, in the garden
there are flowers, blue and yellow.
Go and pick me two big bunches."

Giggling, nudging, off they scampered
and we had our final meeting.

Back came Rhys and little Phoebe.
"Sandra, Sandra, look!" they said.
We have picked you lots of flowers,
lovely flowers, blue and yellow,
to put in water, by your bed.

Suddenly, the place was empty,
gone the grownups. Gone the children
with the laughter they had come with,
but the joy – they left behind.

What a lovely summer evening!

2001

11

Jostling with the Pears

This is the time of year when the fruit trees begin to assert their rightful place in our gardens. Spurred on by the rain and sun (we have to accept the ration that is meted out) the fruits swell, so that the shine on them is better visible. My grandchildren, on visits, watch and wait eagerly for the scrunching days to dawn. So do the birds! The latter have had more than their fair share of the black, white and red currants on the few remaining old bushes, and I never did get a chance to sample the blueberries on a bush newly planted in Spring, even though I put it in a sheltered corner and (I thought) netted it securely. Next year, I contemplate sleeping in the garden during berry-fruiting times, to get my fair share of the produce.

But I can't grumble. When we moved to Pear Tree Cottage, twenty-seven years ago, Angus, my eldest, hover-mower-ed the two-foot high grass and I (younger and stronger then) dug much of the one-third-acre garden and treated it with manure from Stan Ruff's farm, up the lane. Subsequently, it was manured every year for about the next fifteen years, then, every other year, until the soil was so friable that it is positively exciting to scoop up a handful and let it trickle richly through one's fingers.

One of the first things (pardon, beings!) I planted, was a Conference pear tree. It seemed the appropriate thing to do, given the name of our cottage. I was told later that I should have planted two, to fertilise each other, so it wasn't surprising that the harvest of pears for the next three years was poor.

"Cut it down, Angus!" I said, "It's not worth leaving it there. Duly, he sawed the tree down to about a foot from the ground, and we thought no more about it. However, the tree had other ideas. The next spring, I noticed odd, spared twigs sprouting leaves. A year later, more twigs, fattening into branches, with more leaves, larger and a brighter green. And so it went on until, at last, the pear tree has truly asserted its claim to attention and admiration, and brought forth prize fruit.

This year, the warmth and rain pleased my pear tree and, by way of thanks to the Provider, the pears are large, shapely, prolific and smooth-skinned. During the growing season, I had given them two sprays of organic, garlic pest deterrent, and that worked.

As I walk up that particular garden path, I enjoy the glistening French beans leaning over from their wigwams and I relish – jostling with the pears.

Summer, 2009

12

Presents

When you had left,
I missed the noise
and laughter of the party.
But it was peaceful.

On the kitchen table
kind guests had put presents.
I opened the chocolates
and was about to pop one in my mouth
when – what did I see?
Clearing away bright wrapping paper –
your flowers for me…

You had come to me, first,
with a small daisy
and a little smile;
then, with a dandelion,
bigger,
with a bigger smile.

Charis means charity, or love.
You *are* love
and those two flowers
were my loveliest presents
of all.

*Written for my beloved granddaughter Charis Saer, after the
Double Celebration at Pear Tree Cottage, Watersfield, on 1 September 2007:
of 25 years living here and 20 years writing and publishing here*

13

Real **True Grit**

For the thousands who watched the Normandy 75th D-Day celebrations on television, the date – 6 June – will have brought back many memories. My own were of Albert Cowser Saer, my late husband.

As a very young lieutenant in the US Navy, Bert was the first to step off his ship on to Omaha beach – and experience all the horrors brought immediately to his sight.

These horrors were recalled by the small cluster of very old D-Day veterans who gathered in Normandy, on that very beach, to be part of this year's key anniversary. Some of them were very old indeed (and, I am told, one died shortly after that grand occasion). We were moved by their memories, and *they* were moved as they recalled them.

Their comments were gentle, some quite profound. Some things recalled, were still very clear in those old minds … The sea they saw when they landed – "pink with blood"; the dreadful carnage that met their young eyes, just as it met those of Bert. One said that although their D-Day experiences were dreadful, those of soldiers currently fighting in Afghanistan were even worse – *they* never know what is going to happen next, and from what direction.

Sprucely dressed, some sporting Para berets, medals pinned to their uniforms, not one of the veterans voiced recrimination or resentment. They had done their job as best they could; the job they had been sent to do.

But I think what struck me most, during that long, splendid programme, was their bravery. Yes, they were brave all those years ago. But this day, in the rain, I thought how marvellous that they had had the courage, the *true grit*, to make that journey across the Channel in order, as more than one put it, "to honour our comrades"! Soon, none of them will be with us any more – how long can nonagenarians go on for?

Not just on Remembrance Days in the future, but *every* day when we think of them fighting against tremendous odds, along with those currently engaged in terrible and frightening combat,

We *will* remember them.

14

Encounter with an Old Robin

This morning, raining,
he came into the kitchen,
moved around, slowly,
swivelling his head
in a total circle,
the way birds can.

Glazed, half-closed eyes
and matted, shaggy feathers
proclaimed his age.
His faded breast
was the red of
'Old MacGregor' tartan.

I was trying to eat.
No matter.
This was a situation I had to meet,
there and then.

"Come on," I said,
"come out!"
(A perk of the ruffled head)
"You need to eat."

Beyond the cottage door
I threw some seed.
Reluctantly, the robin
left the warmth of the kitchen

and stood beside me,
considering the meal...

Next time I went out
The seed still lay, untouched,
on the damp ground.
There was no sign of him.

Friendship appears
in all shapes and sizes.

This was written long before I worked on Andrew Lack's book, REDBREAST The Robin Life and Literature. *With no ulterior motive, I emailed it to him, hoping to cheer him, on another rainy morning. He emailed back:. 'It did! It's going in Chapter 1!')*

15

Once upon a Time

Once upon a time in America? No, this is about once upon a time in our own country. We used to be Great Britain, but sadly only some have 'GB' on their cars now. But we all have our GB memories.

We who were Wartime Babies had many difficulties but many pluses in our daily life. It was all so much less complicated then. A little known but great writer called Austin Dobson wrote, in a poem called 'Country Life':

> 'The easeful days, the dreamless nights,
> The homely round of pure delights,
> The calm, the unambitioned mind
> Which all men seek, and few men find.'

My own childhood was spent in a little village in North Wales, called Pen-y-ffordd, not far from Gladstone's Hawarden – and Roger Moore's Mold. We lived in house which, when re-visited, seemed incredibly small for two parents and three children. My mother had to cook in an oven governed – and I mean, governed! – by the heat of an open kitchen fire. Scarlet-faced but determined, she produced wonderful Sunday roasts, and we all helped her peel the vegetables, chatting round the kitchen table, before they were put in pans to boil on the open fire.

One Sunday, my mother not being well, I walked alone, aged seven, down the village street, bound for the corrugated shack which was our Church of England place. On the way, I had to pass the Primitive Methodist Church. From inside came the sound of rich Welsh voices, singing a hymn in harmony.

'Mmmm,' I thought, 'I'll go in there.'

I walked without further hesitation into the building (brick-built and not at all 'primitive') and was greeted by two men, all smiles.

"Hello, love," one said, "come to us this Sunday, have you?"

"Yes," I said, shyly, "I – I like your singing…I like to sing myself."

"Then come and sing with us. Maybe you'll sing a solo?"

The Service was a happy, hearty one. They asked me to choose a hymn I liked, and sing a verse from it. I chose *All things bright and beautiful*, and sang the verse about 'the purple-headed mountain'. (From my bedroom window at Tanglan Cottage, I could see the peak of *Moel Fammau*, so this verse seemed right.) I don't think I sang very well, I was too nervous, but everyone clapped!

Afterwards, in a room at the back, people were signing a large book. I asked what they were writing.

"They're signing The Pledge, duck," said a a pretty, fat woman in a floral dress.

"The Pledge? What is that?"

Mrs Floral Dress smiled. "They're signing to promise not to drink alcohol ever, or ever again. Would you like to sign?

I thought hard. "No, I don't think I will."

"Why not?" another woman demanded, sternly (not at all as nice as Mrs Floral Dress).

"Well, when Mummy is getting Sunday lunch ready, when she has put the roast in the oven, I have a sip of her sherry, and I like it."

Also from the age of seven, I had to get up at 6.30, breakfast, then walk alone a mile and a quarter to catch the train for a ten-mile journey to Wrexham. There, I walked another half mile to get to the Convent High School. Then there were the journeys back again. In winter, it was dark when I went to get the train.

It was all very routine, very peaceful. I never thought of complaining – and it must have made me very fit! Sometimes my mother met me, if she felt well enough, with Chips, our mongrel dog.

Would any of us risk sending our children or grandchildren on such a trek on dark mornings, or even in the daylight, back again?

Some of you will remember similar treks. In a lovely country book called A SHEPHERD'S DAUGHTER, published by The Window Press, Petworth, in 1987 (the year my book on Coldwaltham also came out) and written by Evelyn Pentecost when she was 82, she describes regular walks with her family from West Burton several miles to the South Downs. There, they would rescue their hidden kettle from under a stone, fill it with water, light a fire, and make tea. After a peaceful sit-together, they would walk all the way home again. Children in wartime were fed adequately, but not extravagantly, thanks to ration books. They had coupons, too, to buy sweets, like 'Uncle Jo's Mint Balls', and peppermint humbugs, really relishing such treats.

For Christmas decorations, we cut and pasted paper chains at school, and these were hung at home by proud parents. (That, happily, still goes on.)

Christmas was totally different, once upon a time. It didn't start in September with fake Christmas trees in the shops, hung with fake, wrapped parcels, and computer-printed labels on them, reading 'Season's Greetings'.

Not until the middle of December did the real seasonal excitement begin. Then, the tree was bought and decorated by the whole family, with gentle squabbles about who would put the Christmas fairy on the tree's top.

My daughter Bella, when ten, wrote this before she went to bed:

POOR FATHER CHRISTMAS

Father Christmas is coming tonight.

Hang up your stocking and turn out the light!

Leave him some wine and a chocolate bis*cit,*

Remember to see that the candle is lit.

Here he comes riding down from the sky...

What is that noise in the sitting room?

Bang!

Ow!

Hear him sigh.

(He fell down the chimney, and started to cry.)

Poor Father Christmas was very upset.

But Jesus was born to comfort all sufferers.

16

You're a Star!

During a Christmas Day lunch with Angus, my eldest son, and his extensive family, I told a story borrowed from the Vicar of Coldwaltham.

At a Service the week before, David recalled that a friend's daughter had been told one Christmas Eve ON NO ACCOUNT to wake anyone early on Christmas morning. She was to wait until everyone was up. (This, because her parents had placed her much-desired present of a bike under the tree and they didn't want her to find it before breakfast.)

Needless to say, at around 6 am the little girl rushed into their room.

"Mummy, Daddy, come quick! (Oh dear, they thought, she's seen the bike and the pleasant surprise is lost.)

Her parents were peeved but gave in, and followed her reluctantly downstairs into the sitting room. Astonished, they watched her run to the window, totally ignoring the unwrapped bike (How do you Christmas-wrap a bike?!).

"Look, look," she cried, nose pressed to the glass. Look – up there! It's the Star of Bethlehem!"

Sure enough, a star, mellow gold in a lightening blue sky, was still brightly shining.

In a world we tend to regard as totally materialistic, it is good to be jolted into realising that not everyone is obsessed by personal possessions all of the time.

Children are moved by simple things. If properly and lovingly taught, they will show their elders (not always their betters?) what is what, straight from the shoulder.

I like to think that the telling of my story that Christmas Day in Oxfordshire affected the large gathering, not just then, but on…

Next day, Boxing Day, eating again *en famille*, I asked one of the children to pull a cracker with me. She looked away and went on chatting to a cousin. Saddened, I went back to eating lunch.

A little later, there was a slight tap on my arm. Charlie, one of the children, was standing beside me, cracker in hand.

"Will you pull my cracker with me?" he asked, with a small smile.

He had watched the other child turn away and saw a chance to cheer me up.

And he did!

17

Winter comes ...

Winter comes, slowly,
unexpectedly
(not always welcome)
out of autumn.
Rogue frosts sneak down, searing
the last of the beans
hanging-on for picking, in the garden.

The old find the cold difficult to bear,
retreating inside to
reassuring warmth, and bed.

Winter comes, quickly, cruelly,
to the aching heart.
Cold replaces the heat
of love known, then lost.

Yet winter has winning ways –
cosy evenings, in this cottage;
a log fire lit and warming.
The Rayburn, too,
now has its *moments de gloire*:
heating, cooking; bringing back to life
freezing fingers, just in
from bean-pod foraging.

And the real plus?
The coming of Christmas!

Winter comes.
Soon, though,
my mother's first snowdrops
will certainly appear
(They do so every year.)
and Spring will come.
It's just a God-step behind.

This was the last poem I wrote at Pear Tree Cottage.

What they wrote about

MORE FROM PEAR TREE COTTAGE

from Reviews

'It's a cruel world, and this collection of…reflections, poems and essays, presents us with a therapeutic glace at a gentler view of life.

'Sandra's … highly personal faith-based musings (are) from her cottage and garden at Watersfield in West Sussex, where she "wanders mentally footloose" to record her impressions in a stream of consciousness.

'The result is a charming miscellany…, in which the author looks at life from the perspective of the domestic round, mingled with references to a wider world.' *(Freddie Lawrence,* THE ARGUS)

'Nothing can beat a feeling of love shared with others.'

'With the 1998 original book, FROM PEAR TREE COTTAGE, now out of print, this follow-up volume incorporates that book and includes a whole new collection of thought-provoking writing.

'Many of the pieces are likely to give considerable pause for thought, whether reflecting on "Church is where the warmth is", or pondering "Pin-striped passions". …

'A true joy.' *(David Guest,* CHICHESTER (Diocesan) MAGAZINE)

A Personal Testimonial

'A gem of a book, packed with homely wisdom – the blessings of life in the countryside, a cottage garden, fellowship of family and friends, and all the little things that make life so worthwhile: smiles, kindness and love. Sandra's inspirational message is full of the sheer joy of living.'
(Kim Leslie, WEST SUSSEX RECORD OFFICE)